paramour

a collection of poems

by Rebecca Routh-Sample

ISBN 978-1-4457-9577-5

Published 2024 by Lulu Press Inc

9 781445 795775

Other books by Rebecca Routh-Sample

Fiction

Diary Of A Teenage Fangirl

Diary Of A Teenage Rebel Girl

Poetry

ghost world

donnie darko

paramour

Spinner's End

The Greatest Love Story Never Told

If You're Reading This, I Have Some Questions

paramour by Rebecca Routh-Sample

All available to purchase on www.lulu.com
and www.Amazon.com

Connect with me on social media if you want! I'd love to hear your feedback:

Twitter: @itsbeccafy

Instagram: @beccafyofficial

TikTok: @itsbeccafy

contents

19. human life
20. red letter day
21. brand new shoes
22. truly, madly, deeply
23. bluebird
24. a mother's love

crush

she was like candy she
tasted so sweet
tattoo scar on your ribs
two left feet lonely hearts
column your advert i see
'an old flame looking for a
summer fling' but i fell down
the rabbit hole i was so high
i didn't feel a thing i was
searching for my sanity
where is my mind? what
happened to my life? heart
shattered into several million
pieces sea glass
kaleidoscope looking
through the remains pain,
pain, pain crush, crush,
crush and you have the
nerve to ask me out for
lunch?

forever, always,
everywhere

he was like rain
he was apple-bobbing and picture frames he
was my best friend
he was the comfort of your duvet when the day
ends

he was my small town he was
knowing he'll turn up when no
one is around he's the half
moon
he's the only person in the world that
understands you

he was pain
that slow dull ache at the end of a long day
he was everything he was my
best-laid plans he was singing to
Drops of Jupiter dancing
around in his pants

he was the universe planets,
stars, the moon
he was sunshine, darkness, spring, autumn,

summer, winter, cool

he was the end of the day and
the beginning of the day he
was always there reliable,
dependable
forever, always, everywhere

goodbye, to you

don't come around here with that
sadness take my frozen heart and
thaw it out in the blackness hang out
with your friends go ahead, hang out
with your friends but don't expect
me to be home when the night ends
you know i can do better? much
better than you but we
have history, heart, memories and
truth

and if that isn't good enough
than fine hello, to me
goodbye, to you

serial killer

i found love in the heart
of a stranger i felt a love
that was real
as yours became faker
i fell in love will a serial killer and
he got better as i got sicker
i don't even want to try
anymore walk right
past my
locked front door

i used to have dreams of you
being with me but then you
decided to leave stepping off the
platform whisked away
up north
in a storm

if you loved me you'd fight
to stay you wouldn't say
'fuck you' you wouldn't walk
away but the money is
good and the money is
right and the money won't
keep you up at night?

but what about me? what
about everything we used
to be?

i love you

in the night i remember my trauma but in
my days i drown in you
i live fervently and
fearlessly like i'm rookie
blue
but in the night i live in longing,
despondence and uncomfortable truth like
i'm moody blue but then i wake up in the
morning and bask in the light of you drink
coffee and make love to you like i don't
remember what i used to do before you i

love you, i love you, i love you to death i
love you, i love you, you're my best friend i
love you, i love you, i love you times ten
but don't you ever dare leave me again

girl in a bar

there's no such thing as bad girls
just interesting girls we're not a
collective although we try our
hardest we're all different no two
are the say you say 'i hate women'
okay?

watch some jordan peterson
and cry into your noodles go
and pray to god and ask to be a
chad curse all the girls that are
'bad' it won't get you
anywhere good anytime

if you don't love women, poor you i'm
a sapphic so you know i know the truth
if you don't know any women, go
meet some be a decent person and

maybe you'll have some fun there's
more to life than bartering and power
maybe
you'll find your best
friend stay up all
night talking for
hours maybe you'll
find your other half
and your heart will glitter with stars the only
way it starts is
talking to a girl in bar

who will be there?

who will be there when the sun
meets the sky? when the water
runs dry? when every last person
you know begins to die why do
you make it so damn hard? do
you take pleasure in gluing back
together the pieces of my broken
heart? do you enjoy decimating
my soul? do you enjoy opening
your mouth wide and eating me

whole? why are you making it so
damn hard? we were always
together right from the very start
don't you think everyone gets
depressed? wanting more out of
life but getting much less? so what
do you expect of me, and you, and
I? and this barren Northern land,
the grey sea and smog-filled sky? i
thought the light was in you and i?
sunset, rainbow, kaleidoscope
heart? refracting over the dullest
ghost world not knowing how
deep our love goes? roots
dampened in soil, rain and snow?
expecting me to always find a way
to save the day? full of resolve and
vigour? angelic enough to avenge
any sinner is that my purpose? is
that my job? or do you just like
putting me through a lot? soon the
end will come it's in my nature to
cut and run but i will stay in this
one horse town until i run that
horse into the ground what was
lost, now is found i'm not letting
anyone else down

Tetsuo's soliloquy

i put the fun in funeral i put the misery
in mis en scene you could be a great
comedic actor but you're a really shitty
friend they sing their lungs out like
sirens i want to die of this virus as she
writhes on the television and
underneath your sheets i'm just
another person being committed over
instagrams and tweets did the
renaissance painters have to drown
out the noise of tiktok? no so why do i
have to hit the books like a bohemian
when you're just blowing smoke? i
could write my magnum opus maybe
you'll write a joke maybe i'll die young
by suicide and you'll get old and croak
in a hospital ward all alone looking left
to right what the hell have i done?
how is this my life? i could have el
dorado but i have copper and knives i
could have had the greatest love of
the 21st century

but i have a perfume saleswoman
for a wife what i have done? i was
so young?
did i had a little too much
fun? this love is hollow like a
vase i feel like i'm insane i'm
like tetsuo and their doing
experiments on my brain
akira, let me go let me go let
me go
let me go home

green light

amusing, mister muso got
that magic, alex russo what
we been through so
monumental a statue,
transcendental of the love we
had that love we lost i would
have protected our union at
all costs down on my knees
repent the pentecost i held
you in my arms but your

body dropped don't drag me
down with
you after everything we've
been through

oh like the palms of your hands
i read you like scripture like a
torn up body in the continuum is
a fissure in the story of my life
you're the fixture you're the
green light, the bay the great
gatsby and the mister

i could just tell you lies but i cannot
look in those eyes and pretend
that i'm not drowning

anxious attachments

am i too damaged to ever be
loved? every time i leave my cave i
get a thousand cuts every word a
pin every jab a knitting needle every
opinion a curveball every
conversation a nessecary evil my
attachments are anxious avoidant

and just plain weird i'm on the
wrong medication my dreams filled
with subconscious fears will i ever
leave my parents home
my parents don't even live here
anymore decomposing bodies
but the memories linger   like
smoke hanging in the air laying
in bed in my underwear take-
out pilling up dishes unwashed
life? or just bad luck?

most people have the problem of
not having the talent or success
but my problem is my magic is too
strong for me to possess i'm
remissed to think i'll be my only
friend nobody will ever hear the
deepest symphonies of my
conscience what's wrong with me?
maybe i'll never know but at least
when i'm dead and buried
you'll all exactly know

paramour

a manipulator will manipulate
until there are no emotions
left to fake they'll take the
knife out of you and say
'why'd you hit your own face?' just
to spite your nose? you're so out
of control a narcissist
will bait the borderline until they
explode and they tell all of their
friends and say they need some time
alone until your break-up is blasted
on every single phone and
everywhere you turn someone
whispers the poetry of the lessons
you need to learn when all of your
life you worked so hard
for all the trust you've ever earned and you
can't land punchlines if the audience is
disturbed and the lines you wrote become
ineffable are you real, or something
transcendental?
because how do you know someone
else if you don't know yourself you feel
like the dog-eared misshapen

paperback you wish you'd left on the
shelf but what you don't know
is a kid decided not to take their own life because
of you a mother understands their son and lets
them shine without blocking their view and that
radiance radiates on you the scars just show
how much you've been through something real
is worth fighting for
i felt the same way since
the day you knocked on
my door paramour

deuxmoi

and i thought i was doing
alright until you came
along and messed up my
life fading tattoos dark
brown eyes a smile that
only makes me want to
die and you collect
women like trading cards
i look to spade for the

answers talk to me,
deuxmoi who are you to
me?
i still feel twenty three
talk to me tell me i'm the
only one run
around and have your fun
i'm only in love til
the movie is done

i finished in it up
scraping the bottom of the
barrel the movie is
done

alive

in my death was
the only time
i felt alive

i pulled up to my birthday party in a herse
everyone finally felt like they recognised me

and they lit the candles and they all cried and
they all followed me
and gave me likes

before i was a ghost you
never would have known
around all these people i
felt so alone head out on the
open road with a knife so my
throat and i sobbed and
cried until my throat was dry
but you left me there at the
side of the road in a Tuscon
chevy nearing overdose
and if i had any sense i
would've drove as fast i can
but your reality is easily
distorted by an evil man
and my mother and father
well, they never knew and
your mother and father were
one of a special few who
don't feel remorse when
they end you
murder, murder, kill

paramour by Rebecca Routh-Sample

'baby, it's fine as long as
you get home in time
don't stay up fast curfew
it's okay if she hurts you
just let her know you'll
end her life next time
you're gonna drive'

so many girls
don't know if the
next drive
will be their last drive
so many mothers wave goodbye
not knowing
if their daughter will come back
alive

what a time to be alive

love and death (both feel like drowning)
i see you down every single street and every
single hallway and every single doorframe every
single night and behind each door
it's always gonna be you

bad tattoos, broken scars
the look in your eyes
wistful but full of mourning
arms holding me drowning
slowly into infinity at the
bottom of the pool arms
reaching out to me it's
you in a suburban lunch
box town running into your
arms every time
i come around

i'm missing you when you're
right beside me i'm lonely
when you're a few blocks away
i call you at 2am to see if you
want a takeaway three knocks
on the door and you're here to
stay my oldest, dearest friend
i'm only one call away from the

paramour by Rebecca Routh-Sample

deepest, sweetest death
swallowing me whole but the
emergency contact in my
phone messing up my whole
life depression, like a riptide
and the light off of the bay is
emerald somehow the kind of
green that's mean and you
don't think twice about jumping
in

i had a lucid dream last night
you were walking on water and a
girl stood next to me was
condescending
acting like she knew you like i
do but you kissed me on the
face and took me to the bowling
alley above the arcade we had a
shotgun wedding escaping the
fray we drove over the wily,
windy moors all the way home
clicked my heels
and home

tavi

tavi lived in a crayon cardboard box filled
with the hopes, dreams and mood rings of an
army of misrepresented youth that just
wanted to be seen and the rookie of the year
had to be me i wasn't awake enough to
implement those rose-coloured glasses to
my reality
sure i wanted pastel pink paint picket fences
and daisy chains a wish on each petal to live
in a different place i read her essays like a
preacher practicing scripture reading aloud
my weak spots to a chorus of men and boys
who candidly, did not give a shit a polaroid
collecting abuse and abuse after another
i put those snapshots in a shoe box
and hid under the covers i wanted to
live in the big bright apple i was
trying to figure out who i was, trying
sample after sample of people whose
purpose in life seemed to be leaving
my heart trampled
and in the media i looked for an

example but they just told me they were
bad apples
i want to be karlie, ella, tavi, and taylor
and when i was the biggest mess i ever made
i felt like a failure i was
stuck in a paper town and it
was ripping me in two
until i found out the same thing had happened
to you politically incorrect older man adultery
and crazy fans so if it happened to you
i guess it means it happened to to me too
and i'm so sorry that happened to you if i
can happen to you

scars

scarred me like a tattoo scars
covered by tattoos i'm not the
only person who understands
you let me tell you there's
people who love you and those
that are simply
mistaken

take me as i am and i'll take you as you are
i'll sing along while you drive the car from the
wilderness into a lonely misty island maybe
it's not that pretty but it's warm and inviting
maybe i'm not that pretty but i'm warm and
inviting

prophet

you can ruin and make my day
at the same time

you can ruin and make my life at
the same time

i would kill and maim for
you lobotomise my brain
for you
i'd wait in the rain for you
write a million songs for you

and i'm not even being hyperbolic you're my
muse, and my cure, and my gin, and my tonic
you're everything i've ever known and you're
my prophet

you can get me high off
your supply
of that
sunshine

bitter

i'm not bitter
i'm just twisted

i'm not sour
i'm just not sweet

i'm not your saviour i won't sweep
you off your feet

but i'll be at the end of the phone
whenever you need me if you're in trouble
you will hear me

paramour by Rebecca Routh-Sample

and if i loved you you'll
never leave me keep you
in a heart-shaped locket
for safe keeping the man,
the myth, the legend
my soul, my heart, my reverent **human life**

sew your heart to mine
present, in your eyes
blinded by the sight
enveloped into my
consciousness and being i
know just what i'm seeing if
it's not a love for the ages
babe, i'm not interested
interrogated, but i don't need
to explain anything to
anyone you are my one the
only thing money can't buy
is human life

you can't recreate the fragments
of your mind can't create the
fractals of blue in your brown
eyes
a first kiss
you've never known a love like this

paramour by Rebecca Routh-Sample

you don't know what you got until it's gone

i love you to the moon and back

red letter day

i'm never gonna waste another
summer
i won't take for granted
another lover i'm never
gonna wait for another
moment to be over i'm never
gonna anticipate
being older

i want this moment to
last forever your
hands in my hands
wearing your sweater
layed on your body

paramour by Rebecca Routh-Sample

together forever i
know you should've
read my red letter

when you know better
believe me, you do better
like a cacophony of
regrets and
transgressions you can't
relive a moment it's
gonna forever only god
decides who lives and
who stays together and
it's normal to feel it
means you're alive
it's okay to give yourself a
moment
each day to let yourself cry
but you need to live before
you die for the people you
love
and for every star in the sky

now i know today
is a red letter day
all my fears i'll try
to wash away

the sea is blue
and the sky is
grey every day
spent with you
is a red letter
day

i don't ever want you to leave me
but i know you have to go i know
like each knot in my throat but the
ribbons that tie us stronger than
marigolds i'll go when i go and i'll
know
everything i've been told

it's better on the other side but
you need to cherish
being alive

brand new shoes

i miss you and i miss you
all the damn time like
you're my darling, and
i'm your clementine hand
full of peach pits feel a
kind of melancholy only
quenched by lemon and
lime when i was young i
didn't know if i preferred
the seaside or being lost
in the snow
but now i know

i never knew what i'd really need like
taylor said, when you're young they
assume you know nothing i hope
you don't mind a girl who decided to
make you my muse cut off my hair
and tied my brand new shoes

paramour by Rebecca Routh-Sample

truly, madly, deeply

do you think it's
easy? for me to see
you with HER? do
you think it's easy
pretending i'm not
hurt? screw you and
every single thing

you've ever put me through

so you think you're
gonna take my life with
second hand smoke? so
you think you're gonna
try and bankrupt me by
going for broke?
so you think you're gonna
screw me over by screwing
someone else? make me
think i'm second place by
leaving me on the shelf?
how many narcissists are you gonna date
before you take care of your mental health?

i'm a borderline you cannot
put anything past me
because i feel the wounds
i feel the wounds far too
deeply

bluebird

singing to the girl i once was
singing to the girl i want to be
singing to my past drowning in
the deep blue sea that girl
can't come back she's gone i
heard her final swan song a
bluebird trapped in a golden
cage screaming her own
name wanting to be saved
raven take me the midnight moon

paramour by Rebecca Routh-Sample

a mother's love

a mother's love knows
no bounds it
envelopes you from
the inside out the last
words before my death
a hand reaches out an
untimely lament but
you never ever once
stopped fighting for me
you thought of me
every new year's no
justice no relief for half
a century but i never
had a doubt
you never stopped loving me

you never stopped fighting for me   sleet snow
rain that old back lane on the day miles away
you never wavered for a minute
you never had to admit it

your mother's love enveloped
me

paramour by Rebecca Routh-Sample

ISBN ISBN 978-1-4457-9577-5

Copyright 2024 by Rebecca Routh-Sample

Published 2024 by Lulu Press Inc

9 781445 795775